Milly, Molly
Magic Muffins

"We may look different but we feel the same."

"Outcha come… outcha come… outcha come… out."
"Aunt Maude's a magician," whispered Milly and Molly.

"Outcha come… outcha come…outcha come… out."
"Stop," cried Milly and Molly.

"Horrors," shrieked Aunt Maude.
"If these muffins stick, I'll have you to blame."

"Outcha come… outcha come…outcha come… out." And out they popped. A dozen perfect muffins.

"Magic," sighed Aunt Maude.

"You are a magician," squealed Milly and Molly.

"Oh no I'm not," snapped Aunt Maude. "My chant never fails to deliver perfect muffins. That's all there is to it."

"Off with you," she snipped. "And eat these on the way to school. They'll keep you awake in class."

Milly and Molly sat up straight in class and knew all the answers. But Humphrey slipped off to sleep in his seat.

Miss Blythe had stern words with him after class. "Humphrey," she warned. "You simply must eat breakfast."

"Come with us tomorrow," whispered Milly and Molly.

"Outcha come… outcha come…outcha come… out."

"Aunt Maude's a magician," whispered Humphrey.

"Outcha come … outcha come … outcha come … out."

"Stop," cried Humphrey.

"Horrors," shrieked Aunt Maude.
"If these muffins stick, I'll have you to blame."

"Outcha come... outcha come... outcha come... out." And out they popped. A dozen perfect muffins.

"Magic," sighed Aunt Maude.

"Now off with you," she snipped. "And eat these on the way to school. They'll keep you awake in class."

Milly, Molly and Humphrey sat up straight in class and, this time, Humphrey knew all the answers.

"Well done, Humphrey," congratulated Miss Blythe. "You ate your breakfast."

"I ate Aunt Maude's magic muffins," grinned Humphrey. "Aunt Maude's a magician."

"Aah ha," said Miss Blythe knowingly.
"The magic's in the eating not in the muffin,
you know."

Humphrey wasn't so sure Miss Blythe did know. But he never missed another breakfast. He liked being top of the class!

And Milly and Molly chanted "outcha come… outcha come… outcha come… out", every time they made muffins.

But their muffins didn't always pop out perfectly, which made Milly and Molly think there was something magic about Aunt Maude's muffins after all.

Perhaps she really was a magician.